THE COOLEST JOBS ON THE PLANET

WILDLIFE PHOTOGRAPHER

Gerrit Vyn

Raintree

Raintree is an imprint of Capstone Global Library Limited, a company incorporated in England and Wales having its registered office at 7 Pilgrim Street, London, EC4V 6LB – Registered company number: 6695582

To contact Raintree please phone 0845 6044371, fax + 44 (0) 1865 312263, or email myorders@raintreepublishers.co.uk. Customers from outside the UK please telephone +44 1865 312262.

Edited by Nancy Dickmann, Adam Miller, Laura Knowles, and Helen Cox Cannons
Designed by Richard Parker
Picture research by Mica Brancic
Originated by Capstone Global Library Ltd
Production by Vicki Fitzgerald
Printed and bound in China by CTPS

ISBN 978 1 406 25980 3
17 16 15 14 13
10 9 8 7 6 5 4 3 2 1

British Library Cataloguing in Publication Data
Vyn, Gerrit.
    Wildlife photographer. -- (The coolest jobs on the planet)
    1. Wildlife photography--Juvenile literature.
    2. Wildlife photographers--Vocational guidance--Juvenile literature.
    I. Title II. Series
    778.9'32-dc23

Acknowledgements
We would like to thank the following for permission to reproduce photographs:
Alamy pp. 15 (Enlightened Images/© Gary Crabbe), 20 (© blickwinkel/Poelking); Gerrit Vyn pp. 4, 5, 6, 7, 9, 10, 12, 13, 16, 17, 18, 19 top & bottom, 21, 22-23, 24, 25, 26, 27, 28, 29, 30, 31, 34, 35, 36, 37, 38, 39 top & bottom, 40, 41, 42-43, 44-45, 46-47; Getty Images p. 11 (Archive Photos/Field Museum Library); John Shaw p. 14; Nancy Ostertag p.11; Shutterstock pp. 32 (© Monkey Business Images), 33 (© Vuk Vukmirovic).

Background design images supplied by © Apirut, © Brian Weed, © cobalt88, © cobalt89, © Dhoxax, © donatas1205, © dundanim, © Eky Studio, © Ghenadie, © Gordan, © Skocko, © slashmanche, © Slobodan Zivkovic, © STILLFX, © szefei, © Taiga, © Tjeffersion, © wong yu liang.

Cover pictures of (front) meerkats using a human as a sentry post reproduced with permission of Getty Images (Barcroft Media/Will Burrard-Lucas); (back) of a great grey owl chick calling reproduced with permission of Gerrit Vyn.

Every effort has been made to contact copyright holders of material reproduced in this book. Any omissions will be rectified in subsequent printings if notice is given to the publisher.

Disclaimer

This book is on loan from
Library Services for Schools

www.cumbria.gov.uk/libraries/schoolslibserv

County Council

CONTENTS

THE MAGIC MOMENT

Have you ever wondered whose job it is to take all of those beautiful photos you see of wild animals in books and magazines? Have you wondered what skills it takes to get those photos? Well, I'm here to tell you. I'm a wildlife photographer, and this is the story of how I turned my childhood love of nature into a wonderful career.

FIELD NOTES

10 September 2008, 3.15 p.m., Yukon Delta, Alaska

Today, the red fox finally came out of her den. It was a beautiful vixen and I could hear two young pups whining in the den. She stretched and gnawed on some old bones that were scattered around the entrance. Eventually, she trotted away to look for some real food.

Here I am crouching on the Arctic tundra, waiting for the red fox to appear.

It sounds like a glamorous job, right? But like any job, it's hard work! To get this shot of a red fox, I travelled more than 3,200 kilometres (2,000 miles) from my home to the Arctic tundra with all my equipment. I had to camp for three days, waiting for the cold wind to die down so that I would not be blown over. It was a long and hard journey, but when the fox finally came out of the den and looked at me, it was all worth it.

HOW I GOT STARTED

When I was a child, I was fascinated by nature. I spent every moment that I could exploring the forests, fields, and marshes near my home. I found a lot of cool things outside! I found red-backed salamanders living under logs in the forest; I caught tadpoles in ponds and watched them change into toads; and I chased butterflies through the fields trying to find as many different kinds as I could. I loved the adventure, and every day I would discover something new about nature.

If you want to learn about nature, you have to get out into nature.

DON'T FORGET

Catching small animals can be fun, but can also be dangerous. Always know which types of animals in your area are poisonous and which animals like to bite. When in doubt, don't touch!

If you want to see things up-close and personal, you need a good pair of binoculars. Binoculars magnify what your eyes can see. You'll be able to see animals up-close without getting too close!

Research

When I wasn't outside, I spent a lot of time learning about animals by using field guides. Field guides are books with pictures and descriptions of the different animals and plants in a particular area. I spent so much time looking at my field guides that I would usually know an animal's name the first time I saw it in real life.

All you need to start exploring are some binoculars and field guides.

Learning by observing

One of the best ways to learn more about animals is to watch them closely and to take notes. This is called observing animal behaviour. When I was 12 years old, I began recording my observations in a field notebook, and I still do it today. Learning how different animal species behave is valuable knowledge for wildlife photographers! It helps you to predict an animal's behaviour, and that helps you to be in the right place at the right time so you can get the shot.

TAKING FIELD NOTES

1) Note the date, time, place, and describe the habitat
2) Identify the animal
3) Describe the animal's behaviour
4) Think about why the animal is doing what it is doing
5) Can you predict what it will do next?

FIELD NOTES

21 October 2011, 4.05 p.m., Mount Rainier National Park, Washington, USA

An adult black bear crossed the trail ahead of me this afternoon and allowed me to follow it for a while (from a safe distance!). It was concentrating on feeding, and with all of the ripe berries around it was finding plenty to eat. For the most part, it kept its head down while munching on the low blueberry bushes. It wasn't picking one berry off at a time, but grabbing whole branches in its mouth and getting not only berries but some leaves and twigs, too. With winter approaching, he needs to get all the food he can! And fast!

I knew I'd have a chance of photographing a bear on this day because I knew where the best berry patches were from my field notes!

Pursuing interests at school

I learned a lot more about how the world of nature works in science classes at school. In biology, I learned how animals are related to each other, how they evolved, and what makes them work on the inside. In geology, one teacher helped me to start my own rock collection!

I drew this picture of a snowy owl when I was 14 years old.

My favourite classes, though, were my art classes. I liked looking at the world, seeing the colours and the shapes of things. I liked the way that changes in light made things look different. Of course, the things I enjoyed drawing the most were animals. This helped me develop skills that were important to me later as a photographer. I learned about composition and colour, and discovered all the different ways that animals can be depicted. It laid the foundation for my style as a photographer.

Did you know?

Before there were good binoculars, bird artists used to shoot birds so that they could take them home and see their details when they painted them. We don't do that today! Today, most birds are protected, and artists use photographs and observations to make their paintings.

MY HERO!
LOUIS AGASSIZ FUERTES (1874-1927)

Louis Agassiz Fuertes was a famous bird artist. His bird paintings, like the one below, were the best of his time; he was known for painting birds in life-like poses and colours that were true to life. Some of his paintings show birds in their natural environment. This is something I like to do with my photography.

BECOMING A PHOTOGRAPHER

When I was about 15, my dad got a really nice camera, one that a professional would use. It looked like the cameras we use today, but instead of being digital it recorded pictures on film. He showed me how to use it. Sometimes he'd let me take it out on my adventures if I promised to be really careful. I started taking pictures of frogs, turtles, butterflies, and anything else I could find. Every now and then, I would get close enough to a bird or deer for a clear shot!

Not always perfect

Unfortunately, when the pictures were developed I was sometimes disappointed to find that many were blurry or the animal was too small to see. But occasionally I'd get a good one, and I really liked that feeling of capturing a beautiful image of a creature that I loved. And it was a lot easier than drawing – or so I thought!

This is my dad's old camera. I still have it sitting on my bookshelf!

FIELD NOTES

16 June 1995, 2.45 p.m., Capon Bridge, West Virginia, USA

Today, I found an animal I have always dreamed of seeing: an eastern hognose snake! It was crossing the road near the Cacapon River and luckily I had my dad's camera with me. I think I got some great pictures of it before it slithered into the grass.

ESSENTIAL SKILLS

If you want to be a wildlife photographer, it's important that you are happy to spend time on your own in nature. It can sometimes feel scary, but if you are prepared it is a wonderful feeling. Ask your parents' permission first, and don't forget to take plenty of water, food, and a map with you. Always let someone know where you are going and when you'll be back.

How to take great pictures

There are many ways to learn photography. Some people do courses, while others – like me – teach themselves. There are a lot of great books on all types of photography, and you can also learn a lot by exploring the internet. When I got really serious about taking better pictures, I discovered a series of books by a photographer called John Shaw. John's books were full of the same kinds of photos that I wanted to take, and he described just how he took them and what equipment he used.

Putting it into practice

I began practising and trying his techniques, and I got better and better. It's important to find other photographers who do the kind of work that appeals to you. I now have a long list of photographers whose work I admire; I found most of them on the internet.

MY HERO!
JOHN SHAW (BORN 1944)

John Shaw is a professional photographer and author who lives in Oregon, USA. His book, *John Shaw's Nature Photography Field Guide* , is a must-have for anyone getting started in photography. It taught me all the basics of photography and inspired me to take better photographs. Thanks, John!

Did you know?

Many wildlife photographers are self-taught. They didn't go to college or university to learn photography. So, just get a camera and a lens and have a go!

Camera lenses come in a lot of shapes and sizes.

Gearing up

"Wow, that's a big lens!" I hear that a lot from people. But you don't need a big expensive lens to learn photography. A camera, any lens, and your creativity are enough to get you started. Photography is about experimenting and making the most of the equipment that you do have.

Eventually, though, you will want more lenses and other accessories that will help you take a wider variety of pictures. Unfortunately, lenses and accessories are hard to afford, especially when you are younger. They are a photographer's biggest equipment expense.

Buying lenses

TOOLS OF THE TRADE: TRIPOD

A tripod is one of a photographer's most important tools, especially when shooting with big heavy lenses. It supports the camera and lens, which means fewer blurry images. I use a tripod for almost all of my photographs.

When I was in college, I began saving money so that I could buy more camera lenses. It was a slow process, but by buying things one at a time over many years I got to know how to use each lens well. Another way to save money is to buy used lenses. Just make sure that the lens is in good working order, it fits your camera, and that you are buying from a reputable seller.

DON'T FORGET!

Carrying equipment is hard work. My biggest lens is a 600 millimetre telephoto and it weighs 7 kilograms (15.4 pounds) when attached to my camera. And don't forget you also need to carry a heavy tripod for that. You've got to stay fit if you want to carry that around all day!

I used a macro lens to photograph this Spotted Salamander up close.

What lenses do

Lenses allow you to take any kind of photo you want to and to be creative with how you show your subject. Different types of lenses do different things. Here are the three main types:

- A macro lens lets you take close-up photos of things that are very small, even an insect's eyes.
- A telephoto lens magnifies things that are far away so that you can show a distant animal such as a lion up-close.
- A wide-angle lens can record an entire broad landscape, even wider than your eyes can see.

Sometimes you can use all of these types of lenses to take photos of the same animal. This gives you lots of room to be creative. You can focus on just the details of an animal or show the whole animal in its wider environment.

Showing animals in their environment or just a big landscape is what a wide-angle lens is for.

You wouldn't want to get too close to a lion! I used a big telephoto lens for this one!

Note to self

Having great lenses doesn't mean you'll automatically take great photographs. Each lens has its own strengths and capabilities, and learning what those are is part of becoming a great photographer. In order to be creative, you need to practise with each lens so that you know what it can do.

MAKING A LIVING

These days, with enough hard work, almost anyone can become a good photographer. The recent advances in digital technology have made it much easier for people to take consistently good photos, and the internet provides loads of great resources for learning. That's the good news!

The bad news is that with so many amateurs taking good photos, it has become much harder for people to earn a living from it. It was always a hard profession to get in to, but now it's much harder to earn enough money to live.

Note to self

I am very lucky to have found a career that combines the two things I am most passionate about: nature and art. It was a long road to get here, but it was worth it!

There are a lot more amateur wildlife photographers now than there used to be.

From amateur to professional

After college, I had a lot of other jobs where I earned money to support my photography business as it grew. I was fortunate later to find a unique job at an institution called the Cornell Lab of Ornithology. They hired me to film, record sounds, and tell stories about birds and nature full time.

Did you know?

Many people study animals for a living. Each job has a different name. A person who studies birds is called an ornithologist. A person who studies mammals is called a mammalogist. A person who studies reptiles is called a herpetologist.

This is the Cornell Lab of Ornithology. It is full of people working to study, conserve, and educate others about birds.

Working with editors

A wildlife photographer's job is to take great photos but it is another person's job – the photo editor – to pick which photos are used. When I finish a shoot, I select a group of images that I think are the best. The photo editor then makes the final selections.

MY HERO!
SUSAN MCELHINNEY

Susan McElhinney is the photo editor for *Ranger Rick* magazine. It is a magazine for children all about animals. She gets to find and pick all of the photos for the magazine. That's a very cool job!

Photo editors know exactly what they are looking for and which photographer to use when selecting photos for assignments.

Some birds, such as these snow geese, migrate thousands of kilometres between their summer homes and their winter homes. If you want to photograph them you need to know where they are!

Assignments

One of the most exciting things about being a professional photographer is that sometimes an editor will send you on a special assignment to get certain shots to illustrate a story. Assignments are exciting, but there is also a lot of pressure to do a really great job – and you will also have a deadline to meet.

To be successful on an assignment, it is important to do research and develop a plan for how you are going to get the shots that the editor needs. I try to learn everything I can about the animal species I am going to photograph and the location where I will be working. I want to know details, such as how the animals behave and where and when they are most active. That way, I have a good idea of what I am going to shoot and how I am going to shoot it in advance.

Working with scientists

One of the best ways to get information about an animal and its location is through collaboration with scientists whose job it is to study that animal. An ornithologist, for example, might observe a single bird or a group of birds for months, or even years, at a time. When you spend that much time with an animal you really learn a lot! By working with an ornithologist who studies a species I want to photograph, I can get the best information possible on where the birds are located and how they behave.

I've had a lot of fun collaborating with scientists, and it's great to have company when you are working in remote places. Sometimes I even get to hold an animal that they are studying.

DON'T FORGET!

When collaborating with scientists, you can sometimes help them, too. As a photographer, you might make valuable observations and your photographs can help them tell important stories about the species they are studying.

My friend Audrey is an ornithologist. Here, she is holding a bird she studies in the winter in Washington State, USA. It is called a black turnstone.

Another ornithologist helped me find the nest of a black turnstone on the Alaskan tundra. What a cute baby!

MY HERO!
JOHN JAMES AUDUBON
(1785-1851)

John James Audubon was a famous American ornithologist and painter. His goal was to paint all of the birds of North America, at a time when much of the continent still hadn't been explored. He recorded detailed field notes about many birds that had never been observed closely before. He also discovered 25 new species.

My job is always different – there is no typical day. This chapter will take you through three different types of day: in the field, in the office, and travelling.

Photographing from a hide

A lot of animals are very secretive and hard to photograph. The best way to get shots is to conceal yourself. When photographing the mating displays of prairie chickens, I set up a hide the day before I plan to shoot. Then I wait for the birds to come to me.

Here I am watching the prairie chickens from my hide.

4.30 am	Time to wake up!
4.35	Check the weather and pack up the car
5.30	Arrive near the hide and hike the last kilometre in the dark
5.45	Climb into the hide and set up my camera and tripod. Now is the time to be very quiet!
6.05	Prairie chickens begin arriving and start to call
7.00	Start taking photos!
10.25	Prairie chickens leave the area
10.30	Get out of the hide and hike back to the car
11.25	Download the photos on my laptop and make extra copies
1.30 pm	Take a nap
4.00	Scout other photo locations and take photos until sunset

FIELD NOTES

14 April 2007, 6.35 a.m.
Fort Pierre National
Grassland, South Dakota, USA

While sitting in my hide watching the prairie chickens, I saw a coyote sneaking through the grass towards the birds. Eventually, one of the birds spotted it, and they all exploded into the air and flew towards the rising sun. Unfortunately, it was too dark to get any photos.

A day in the life: office work

Although I like spending as much time as I can out photographing, the truth is that most of my time is spent doing office work. Locations need to be researched, photographs need to be edited and catalogued, and you have to find customers and deliver images to them.

There are always jobs to do in the office. One of my least favourite jobs is cleaning my gear after a trip.

ESSENTIAL SKILLS

If you are running a photography business, you need to know more than just how to use a camera. You need to learn how to do work like accounting, banking, maintaining a website, and customer service. Like any desk job, organizational and maths skills are really important!

7.00–8.00 am	Get up, shower, and breakfast
9.00–10.00	Teleconference with colleagues at the Cornell Lab
10.00–12.00	Video editing
12.00–1.00 pm	Lunch and a walk
1.00–3.00	Research locations for my next shoot
3.00–4.00	Phone call with photo editor
4.00–5.00	Make a selection of photos and email them to the editor

In the evenings, I'll often spend three or four hours editing photos. First, I get rid of ones that are out of focus or flawed in some other way. When only the best images are left, I make final adjustments on things like colour. Finally, I enter caption information.

Editing photos on the computer is fun, but it is very time consuming. Sometimes I will shoot 10,000 images on one trip!

TOOLS OF THE TRADE: COMPUTER EQUIPMENT

To run programs such as Photoshop and catalogue a big collection of photographs, it's important to have a fast computer and lots of hard-drive space for storing things. You'll need a range of computer programs for both editing and running your business.

A day in the life: exotic travel

Travel can be a big part of being a photographer. When I am on the road, every day can be different. I often get to experience new cultures and meet interesting people who live differently from the way I do. I have worked with many people, from Eskimos in Alaska to villagers in Madagascar. You're often away from your family for long periods of time.

Here are some men who helped me while I was photographing in Myanmar, Southeast Asia.

This is what one of my days in Botswana, in southern Africa, was like.

5.00–6.00 am	Wake up and eat a breakfast of local foods
7.00–8.45	Drive to Savuti Channel and start looking for wild dogs
8.45–9.05	Follow the hunting wild dogs
9.05–10.15	Photograph wild dogs catching and eating an impala
10.15–10.45	Photograph a male lion lying in the grass
10.45–3.00 pm	Go back to camp, have lunch, and take a nap
3.00–3.25	Drive to a watering hole where animals drink
3.35–6.40	Photograph elephant groups as they come to drink
6.40–7.00	Drive back to camp, stopping to look at a puff adder crossing the road
7.00–8.00	Dinner
8.00–9.00	Download photos and make copies
9.00	Go to bed

DON'T FORGET

It is important to be organized when going out on a photo trip. Did you remember to bring extra batteries and something to clean your lens with if it gets dirty? You won't find a camera shop out on the tundra or in the middle of a rainforest!

Being a photographer means travelling with a lot of luggage!

ADDING SKILLS

The digital technology used in computers, cameras, and many other devices we use today changes at an incredibly rapid pace. It seems like something new or better comes along every day. So do new ways of doing things. Just 20 years ago, most wildlife photographers only took pictures to make a living. Today, they are often asked to do much more than that.

Online tutorials are a great place to find help on a wide range of subjects.

DON'T FORGET!

The internet is a great place to learn new skills. There are lots of people out there just like you, sharing information and teaching others what they have learned. Search for tutorials on audio, video, and photography skills you want to learn.

This photographer is recording above a mountain lake.

Other types of media, such as video footage and sound recordings, have become more important to clients because the internet has changed the ways in which people can tell stories. On the internet, a magazine article can come to life with a combination of different types of media, such as photos, video, text, and sound. This is called multimedia. Developing multimedia skills can set you apart from other photographers and get you more work. This is what I have done in my career.

Note to self

Don't be afraid to make mistakes. Experimenting and learning from what you did right or wrong is one of the best ways to learn. Just make sure you keep track of what you did in the first place!

Learning video skills

It wasn't long ago that if you wanted to shoot video you needed a video camera. Today, you can shoot video on cameras that were primarily built to take photographs. In many ways, shooting video and photographs is similar, but there are differences. One is that you can move a video camera while you are shooting to create a variety of effects. A pan is a shot where you slowly move the camera across a scene. A zoom is where you slowly zoom into or away from a subject to reveal something.

Professionals usually use big high-definition video cameras like this to film wildlife, but you can also shoot high-quality video on smaller cameras.

This is called a video timeline. You edit video on the computer by arranging all the shots and sounds in the order you want them to play in your film.

When shooting video, you should always get lots of angles and different perspectives. Shoot the details as well as the big picture. This allows you to build a video sequence that tells a story. Imagine you wanted to show a bird going to its nest and feeding its chicks. What different kinds of shots would you need to make an interesting series of shots that show that behaviour?

ESSENTIAL SKILLS

If you're going to learn to shoot video you should also learn to edit video on a computer. Basic software is not too expensive. It's fun to make short edited films for your friends and family.

DON'T FORGET!

One of the hardest things to do a a photographer is to shoot a sing image that tells a story. With vid you should be thinking of telling story in a sequence of images.

Audio recording

Recording good audio of animals is often as challenging as getting a good photograph. Recording birds is something I really enjoy, and I often get to record bird sounds that have never been recorded before. To get a perfect recording, you have to use a microphone that isolates the sound of the animal. You also have to get really close by sneaking up on it. And you'll need some luck! You need a day when the wind isn't blowing, the mosquitoes aren't buzzing, and there are no planes flying overhead. Sometimes another loud bird can ruin your recording.

Here I am using a parabolic dish to record a bird. A parabolic dish magnifies the sound you want to record.

At the Cornell Lab of Ornithology, we have the largest collection of animal sounds in the world. They are used by scientists studying animal communication, by teachers in classrooms, and even in Hollywood films. Thousands of my bird recordings are catalogued and preserved in the Cornell collection.

Did you know?

The world is a very noisy place. It is almost impossible to find a place without some human-made noise. Next time you're outside, listen to all of the human-made noises that are out there!

This great grey owl chick was really loud, so I didn't have to get too close to get a nice recording. And a photograph!

ESSENTIAL SKILLS

Audio editing is another computer skill that seems hard at first but just requires some practice.

PUTTING IT ALL TOGETHER

Why do all of the skills I have mentioned so far matter? Well, in the end, being a photographer is all about telling stories. And these skills enable you to be a good story-teller in many different ways, both in print and on the internet. If you want people to listen to you, you need to make your stories as engaging as possible. Sometimes your story may be so important you want the whole world to know it. So it had better be good! And that means having the skills to make it good.

Every spring, emperor geese return to the Yukon Delta to nest. This mother has laid four eggs and will keep them warm for weeks.

Emperor goose mothers are very protective of their nests, and will scare off predators by raising their wings and hissing.

FIELD NOTES

3 July 2012, 11.20 a.m., Yukon Delta National Wildlife Refuge, Alaska

This morning the rains and winds finally died down, and I was able to leave my tent and check the emperor goose nest. I could tell immediately from the mother's behaviour that the chicks were hatching. For weeks she has been lying motionless on the nest with her head held low, trying to blend in with the surroundings. But today she had her head up and was active. When I approached, I could see two of the cutest grey goose chicks I have ever seen.

If a mother has cared for her nest well, the young finally hatch and a new generation is born.

Using photography for a purpose

The most fulfilling part of my job comes when I am lucky enough to capture a moment in an animal's life that has never been recorded before, or I get the chance to tell a story that helps to conserve a species. On one assignment, I spent three months in the far north of Russia in order to get the first good photographs, sound recordings, and video of one of the world's most endangered birds – the spoon-billed sandpiper. My work allowed people around the world to see this magical spoon-billed bird with its babies for the first time. I got the satisfaction of knowing my work might help more people to care about it and act to save it.

This is one of the first photographs ever taken of a spoon-billed sandpiper with its chick. I'm really proud of this one!

Here I am with one of my articles about the spoon-billed sandpiper printed in the BBC Wildlife Magazine.
I have a great job!

Saving a sandpiper

FIELD NOTES

12 June 2011, 2.00 p.m., Chukotka, Russia

I have been in my hide near the spoon-billed sandpiper nest for 15 hours, waiting for the eggs to finally hatch. At last, I saw a chick pop out of the nest and stumble and tumble around the nest on its wobbly legs. After a few minutes, it crawled back under its father to get warm. It was one of the most exciting moments of my life!

QUIZ

Take this quiz to see if you have what it takes to become a wildlife photographer.

1. What do you most prefer to do in your spare time?

a)   Play sport
b)   Explore nature and watch animals
c)   Play video games and watch television

2. What appeals to you the most?

a)   Always having a home-cooked meal and a warm bed at night
b)   Being uncomfortable at times if it means you get to go on an adventure
c)   As long as it's indoors, I'm happy!

3. What type of work environment are you looking for?

a)   I'd like to work in an office where I have lots of interaction with other people
b)   I like to rely on myself and work alone for extended periods of time
c)   I like to work in a physical environment where I am mostly using my body

4. How would you describe yourself?

a) Physical and athletic
b) Artistic and creative
c) Someone who gives up easily if something is too hard

5. What is most important to you?

a) Making money and being financially secure
b) Doing something you love, even if it means not having everything you want
c) Focusing most of your time on friends, family, and relationships

If you answered mostly Bs, you just might have what it takes to begin exploring a career as a wildlife photographer!

GLOSSARY

accessory thing that can be added to something else to make it more useful or do something different

accounting keeping track of money that is spent and earned, to make sure that a business is making money

amateur someone who does something as a hobby, rather than as a job to make a living

collaborate to work together with other people to do a project

composition process of arranging the subject matter in a picture so that it is pleasing to the eye

conserve to preserve and protect the natural environment and its inhabitants

continent very large land mass. Earth has seven continents.

deadline date or time by which a project must be finished

den hiding place, for example a hole in the ground, that some animals raise their babies in

edit process of selecting the best photos from a photo shoot

evolve when a plant or animal species changes over a long period of time in a way that makes them better suited to survive in their habitat

field guide book for identifying things such as plants and animals

geology scientific study of the structure of Earth, how it was made, and how it changes over time

hide small tent used to get a close view of animals

macro lens camera lens used to magnify things that are very small

mating display special type of behaviour used by male animals to attract females

migrate to move from one place to another to find food. Many types of animals migrate from one season to the next.

multimedia combining a variety of media types, such as sound, photos, or video, to communicate a story or idea

ornithology the study of birds

pan side-to-side video camera movement used to show a wider area like a landscape

parabolic dish device used to collect and amplify sound for audio recording

photo editor person whose job is to select the best photographs for a product such as a book

species specific type of plant or animal. For example, lions are a species and so are monarch butterflies.

teleconference meeting in which people working on a project communicate from different places by using a telephone or video network

telephoto lens camera lens that magnifies a distant object

tripod three-legged support for holding a camera still

tundra barren, treeless landscape of the far north

vixen female fox

wide-angle lens camera lens that captures a wide view, for example a whole landscape

FIND OUT MORE

Books

Digital Wildlife Photography (John and Barbara Gerlach)

John Shaw's Nature Photography Field Guide, John Shaw (Amphoto Books, 2000)

The above two books are for adults, so you may want to ask an adult to help you when looking at them for information.

Take Great Photos! (Find Your Talent), Adam Sutherland (Franklin Watts, 2013)

There are a number of publishers who make great field guides. You can find guides to trees, birds, insects, and any other wildlife you want to learn about.

Try these publishers for UK field guides

- Kingfisher field guides
- Collins field guides
- AA field guides

Websites

www.allaboutbirds.org
The All About Birds website gives a great introduction to the birds of North America.

www.discoverwildlife.com
BBC Wildlife magazine's website has loads of cool photos and articles about wildlife.

www.gerritvynphoto.com
You can see more of my photography on my website.

www.macaulaylibrary.org

The Macaulay Library website provides detailed information on wildlife sound recording techniques, and you can listen to more than 100,000 recordings of animals made by people like me.

www.outdoorphotographer.com

Outdoor Photographer magazine's website provides lots of helpful articles for photographers.

www.rspb.org.uk/wildlife

The website of the Royal Society for the Protection of Birds is a great place to find out more about birds and other UK wildlife. There is also a section listing nature reserves that you can visit to see wildlife for yourself.

I love looking at the work of other photographers. Good ones all have a unique style. Here are a few of my favourites:

Vincent Murnier (www.vincentmunier.com)

Tom Mangelsen (www.mangelsen.com)

Frans Lanting (www.lanting.com)

John Shaw (www.johnshawphoto.com)

Joel Sartore (www.joelsartore.com)

Topics for further research

If there is an animal in your local area that you particularly like, such as a woodpecker or a squirrel, why not try to identify what species it is with a field guide, observe its behaviour for a week, and write down field notes. If you take photos, make sure to note where and when they were taken. This will be good practice for when you become a wildlife photographer!

INDEX